Who by Water

Kate Ashton

Who by Water

Shearsman Books

First published in the United Kingdom in 2016 by
Shearsman Books
50 Westons Hill Drive
Emersons Green
BRISTOL
BS16 7DF

Shearsman Books Ltd Registered Office
30–31 St. James Place, Mangotsfield, Bristol BS16 9JB
(this address not for correspondence)

www.shearsman.com

ISBN 978-1-84861-480-2

ACKNOWLEDGEMENTS
The poems in this volume first appeared as follows: 'Home Again from Long Ago'
in *Envoi*; 'Tide Turn' in *The New Writer*; 'Waddenzee', a sequence of fourteen
poems with photographs by Gerrit Offringa, on the *Shearsman* web gallery at www.
shearsman.com; 'The Mystery of Glass' in *Shearsman* magazine 83 & 84; 'n' Bytsje'
and 'Half by Half We Sleep' in *Shearsman* 93 & 94; 'Tenebrae' in *Shadowtrain*;
'Gull' and 'Milk Bay' in *Northwords Now*; 'Who by Water' in the supplement to
Agenda, 2016; 'Easter Sunday at Findhorn Bay' in *THE SHOp*; 'Winter's Child' in
Long Poem Magazine. 'She Who Weeps' was published by Lapwing Publications as a
pamphlet entitled *The Concourse of Virgins* (May 2012).

My thanks are always due to Fiona Sampson, who first taught me that I could
write a poem, and to another of her 'October Poets', Janet Sutherland, for her fine
example and encouragement. I am very grateful to Tony Frazer for his continuing
interest in my work.

Contents

For Colin

Half by Half We Sleep

On this eve of nativity
twined lovers stranded high
above tideline on shore
of age-stroked stones a gift,
a present each to each

beneath far rainbow doubly born
of brine, cord cast uncut
into blue noon like diadem
of neonate studded with news
to shake the snow-streaked hills

– and half by half we sleep
watched over by the same veiled nurse
and half by half we wake
to the becoming of the universe.

Tide Turn

April sea running blind
to or from the sun, skirts
filled with light,

to give or take in
their first kiss, to
turn the tide on
double bliss

twice tumbled
twins in ecstasis

strand ruched high
ribbed low by lunar love, no
if and why and when,
first ebb then flow –

only the stone-eyed
viking seal, high-prowed,
ruddered, rowed

rocked dry and
riding time knows
pinioned
momentum,

vertigo,

rode heave of water
in the womb, moon-
clutched dominion

of neither now nor
then or come or go.

Home Again from Long Ago

Home again from long ago
to narrow sparrow-romped close,
honeysuckle laden lane, to wild
white rose and fledgling
fluttered lilac.

Home from flatland exile, wind-spun
horizon without end, to mountain
uttered song deeper and darker
than histories, jasmine's
night shining stars

falling, caught in the cobweb
breath of coming wish come
true, spanning night's secret
rendezvous, northerly ice
calling the tune

of whale locked in some rocky
cave beyond the bay where rain
veils hamlets humped and grey,
remote as memory, lost as
the coracle.

Home again from then, when
childhood's footstep led away
across the rambling railway track,
never to climb the flower-fled,
the flower-bled embankment back.

The Mystery of Glass

My sister has gone outside now.
I do not know if she feels the rain,
sees ragged crow dragging his
frayed feet above the field,
smells clover mead reigned
over by brown kye, crown-
uddered as queens.

Perhaps she walks the clouded hill
with me, watches the firth evaporate,
the crags disintegrate,
the undulating land whisper
its muted antiphon from crypt
to misted crypt crouching
between cached sunshine –

caught between
yes and yes,
a russet hind
hugging tarnished
gorse edge –

maybe she stops to thrust her thumb
into the foxglove maw,
eager to silence that mauve throat
for now or evermore,
its prescience, its deadly
digitalis roar, or runs ahead
to meet the many-faced magenta stare
of rose-bay willow-herb stabbing
honeysuckle-crept floor
where mitred *felix mas*
waves tawny-haired
munificence, broadcasting

dusky spoor where thrush
scatters her ashy unsung song,
soothsaying robin
and slight wren run;

or waits beside harebell-rung
verge where dreamy dissemblies
spin of thistle's burnt-out stars
to watch the swallows harvesting
their dancing wheat-flung
fare in leaping pas de chat,
unearthly, sown in air –

wing

as she
sliding
severing
light diving
dividing
shuddering stalk
from flower a-gawp,
lisping
its scented song
of where
colours
come from

or leaf
in bright diatribe
against the wind's
wild cry
of coming rain,
beside itself
with life

in love
with clandestine
flow of time
hunting oblivion
for fragments
of itself

rain

kissing the street, the
earth, the unforgiving stain,
veil of heaven-sent
remorse, or grief,
missing seen
crystal through
crystal to
crystal bead
upon the ground

a bird
a memory of flight
or origin of height
higher than soprano
shift of tongue, a
touch alit upon
by notes and shine,

into the citrus throat
of toadflax slides
a drop of sky,
parched calyx swallows
wept rebirth
preserving it
until some quaking sun
in passing snaps
and slakes its thirst –

giving and taking
is all we know –

tell me a teardrop
from its wild cousin,
tell me the truth.

(I waited
and you did not come.
Outside a bird
sang my obliteration,
rain fell unendingly
it seemed; night
came and went
and day reconvened

again)

and again I was excluded. Entrances
and exits were made, instructions issued
and laws obeyed; I saw the endless carnival
repeat itself and all of life was spectacle.
Here is the meaning: truth
does not come round again
but is the very constant sustenance.
Do we describe the peril that we do not know
but by hunger and enforced abstinence?

Breaking the bond with fear
is agony. All is still in here.
The clock enunciates its
mannered order, as pre-planned,
as if shared dream
was waking certainty;
the potent march of minutes manned

against contingency. A web
of terror holds in place

the chair, the wall,
the lacquered carapace.
A scream defies the law
whereby each atom may flee
in sudden preference for east,

yet each door opens
upon a furnished void
declaiming its deficiency;
a silent plea for warmth,
occupancy to interrupt
the rage spanning each mute
relationship from ledge to pane.

pain

Today she is tired,
fatigued, she says,
and in the mirror
above the mantelpiece
watches the parade,
the busy business of the street:
devoid of destination, delayed,
foiled by a double act of light
obedient to her need for
more time. The day

is weeping. She waits,
kept in abeyance
by the steepness of the stair,
the self-absorption
of the cat, the sapphire
surface of a tile, square sunlight
listing jasmine. Her
husband is not there.

She waited. Rain
crept down
the window pane
as wept
across porcelain
cheek of denied
Madonna,
led by light,
sky white
holding
her son
oh
lacryma
sistere.

then

Back then, great-grandfather
built his world of glass
(thirteen children
and every one survived) a
shard for every living joy
('the higher up the mountain,
the greener grows the grass')
recalcitrant boy sent
upstairs to his room
('the more a donkey wags his tail
the more he shows his...')
the maid reports to master.

Heart pierced, he knew
(the higher up the mountain)
what his lad saw through.
It was his vocation.
The wonder of it, not
solid nor quite a-flow, the
wealth of it (a bell-pull in
every room), slow
vitrification, great
heat, the memory of sea,
stealthy, manifold solitudes
coalescing yet
not admitting night,
keeping faith with some
forgotten law
transmitted by the tide.

Looking up, he saw
where it all began:
a glittering cascade, a
shuddering, dissembling

span of spectra shattered
in song not of some
wayward child but
belonging to everyone.

face

I was his granddaughter's
darling, her coveted one,
the one she saw in the mirror
each time of day,
each way she looked at me
I was descended from her truth,
the loved, the pirouetting lie
they told. I saw it too.
I was the one
who looked away

to face

and now I am on the street
shuffling like time along
its grey meridian,
my sister somewhere near,
and she whose womb we knew
in great old age lets go
a sudden flood of blood
as if reliving maidenhood,
and then grows young again,
regains vitality, and neither
nurse nor doctor can divine
disease or calculate a cause –

it was her memory,
tripped by the spotted
wally-dog upon her windowsill,
the faded wooden babushka
monitoring her decline from atop
the tv set, the bed that cantilevers
up and down. Trapped
daughters in her lap,
hiding behind her apron,
trying on her headscarf
in the dark, tap,
tapping to come out.

At last we spoke.
'The atmosphere,' she said,
'of one's mind changes.'
I said, 'Don't look at
what I wear.' She said,
'Do I recall correctly

that your son has pale hair?'
I said, 'You should
have been there.'

She turned her head.
'The tree,' she said.

After everyone has gone
she sits on in the space
they leave behind, draped
in another century, struggling
to understand how the same
death has stolen in upon
her twice, and under
the same name.

Sitting at the table
studying the medical
dictionary: stepfather
and now daughter –
what sickness levels
generations without shame?

A frozen fall of light. She wonders
if she should go outside,
if she would recognise
the people that she met,
her kin, the chosen,
the assimilated friend.

She told me once
how time eschewed
the crude perambulations
of the clock, enfolding
each and every age,
sometimes in tenderness,
sometimes in rage;

revealing incidence
where second sight breaks
through (seventh child
of a seventh child). Her
first daughter answers
to her name.

We come and go.
We see what we are shown,
we know what we may know.

now

Long gone the hutted
bodger who turned
and tamed the beech-wood
stave; pale anemone
adrift between his feet,
pignut asleep in
pennoned loamy grave –

above, a cold white weight
hurled at black bark,
the sharp-edged scent
of arboreal blood;
awful pallor upturned
and glistening, as fallen
as a stillborn moon
expressing tears –
too soon, too soon –
between circlets
of hurried youth.

A thousand deaths ascend,
are clasped and carried
to the sea by she
who comprehends
the womb: never
too many, never
too few.

At last set free from light and lead
I watch the stained-glass saints
approach along the orchard path,
running to meet me in the copse

where God made Granny's bentwood chair;
dark-eyed, shedding rainbows they come
with apple-blossom in their hair,
and each one bare-heeled in the grass
where swerving adder lets her pass.

Easter Sunday at Findhorn Bay

Where the soft sea sways in
I walked my anger on the lilac-
shadowed shore; white
feathered tides traversed
and sped the wave

when a west wind flew in
trailing her skirts of brine-
dipped rain, splashing the
stone's dry cheek again
with memories until

the human heart was still,
gave up its livid war
upon the pagan ring, let
go, saw how the wave
arose to swallow acts
of blasphemy and in

its suffering turned blacker
than a bruise, and furies
eddied from the cliff
where sand gives birth
to banded ice-egg quartz
and parched dune gorse

lays down its crown of thorns
and golden tongued hosannas
sings into the storm.

She Who Weeps

Does the land wait the sleeping lord
or is the wasted land
that very lord who sleeps?
                    David Jones

I

The Monastery

Imagine it – I could not look the holy men in the eye; they saw
my breasts and so I caught
                    hold of their dress, clutched at the habit
that they wore and tried to put it on, clung to the hemp, the leather
thong and took to mouthing their doctrine,
                    miming the rituals they dwelt upon. They could
not imagine what I did or why, recalled handmaid and hair-wrapped
feet. Was that cool act
                    of self-abasement, praise, by she who knew
the map of man from head to toe? who let him take her from herself,
caress the last forbidden place,
                    who gave him leave to roam where all the world
of men comes from? Or was it treachery that laid her hand upon
the alabaster box; pourer
                    of sandalwood and shame, bather with night
dancers, those without names? Who could help but fear such
insurrection, rare unction
                    spilled like seed, disruption of the cell
where still she kneels, hands spired, unable to atone for love
that detonates desire.

II
A Gypsy Encampment

We went the long way round to get here – the road of mire and mother
blood. Set off early, though, sure
      of one thing and that was we were right, it was a right
thing we did. At ease, wrapping our waists with wool, we went where we
were led. From girlhood we learned
      the day would come for this following after, and then
the men began settling their eyes on us like flies until we bled, and then
they hung upon our hips until our wombs were full.
      Sometimes their mouths were kind and there were nights
when all we did was welcome them and free of artifice dismay the bed:
wild nights when we remembered what we'd fled –
      the fastness of our fathers' arms and all ways but ways
of fire, finding the old lore scratched on bark, on hearthstone – spore of
saint and magus, priestess, maid and whore,
      she who went ahead. The men amazed us – that we
could steal their strength pretending deference, in meekness catch the
merriment of him and turn it into tears; raise
      and subdue his limbs, confer pleasure as though it were
our special gift and drive the bargain infinitely far– spit out his little
antidotes, strong arm and fist
      and dressing up for war, show sorrowing our wounds
and win the day. The age was done with tales of saviours and snakes.

III
The Concourse of Virgins

Some of us took the veil; some bedded
           others of their kind. In walled gardens we grew into
our vows, cowled and nodding
           promises like prayer. Sometimes we nursed the sick,
until their wounds reminded us
           of how we'd strayed and every hungry hurt clamoured
for love like one betrayed.
           Counting the pulse was chaste, but lesser tending paced
the ward. The men watched our
           approach with knowing eyes, alert to want unsated
by their wives. We bit our lips. We
           smiled. Some higher calling eluded us: in the refectory,
the chapter house and court
           laws were uncovered and explored, while month by
month the moon sent her curved
           claw through thinning skin to clutch at claimed
dominium. We smiled no more,
           disowned the art of anamnesis, signature and herb,
known cure that thrives nearby the cause.
           The barren cell bewitched stood stalled. All freedom
passes into dread, the place
           beyond the portico, unsheltered and unled.

IV
Conspiratio

We have watched from behind the grille, the veil, the way they worshipped,
hiding their heads and covering the face for shame,
           bowing and murmuring their plaints and throwing back
the shawl; beating their breasts and never once turning to see how we
loved them. The tabernacle door,
           the shrouds they drew aside upon the plea: these ways
were never ours, who bathed away our womb blood behind bars and
waited for fecundity. Blessing upon this meat and salt and seven tapers
missing flame, the child, the corpse, the bread and wine,

           and on this kiss –

           before, behind cantor and scroll, serenity, a flare, vivid
but innocent of heat and bare, unclothed of all but bliss that lit silk raiment
and consumed the law, a naked sword
           passing presage into the blood and pouring precedent
where stone had stood before. We wept, we tore our hair. We moaned. The
breath we shared no longer seemed our own.
           It sighed the Psalm abroad as if to hush the name
of war and turned our eyes toward our enemy as though his loss were ours
to see and nothing stood
           between our grace and his iniquity.

V

I ask her who is she
as though she were a foundling girl
recovered from the forest floor
where first frost fires frigid
the fallen leaf and on his cairn
the wild whelp yawns

I ask her once more, who are you?
and still she stares and mouths
her wolfish tongue, gazing idly
into my eyes sidelong, rehearsing
how to run. Hooky cleavers
at her waist. Head hung

VI
Pax

His face the face of the prodigal, wearing his wanderings like forbidden
history, sand-spun anteroom
　　　　　of Bedouin birth, indigo-swept sunset of nomad
smile at sudden death of day, as if he lay down once and let his soul
float free of gravity, the caravan that sways
　　　　　　　　against bedazzled topaz spies his whiteness in sparse
submission to the sky. The one he dreamed he was in life offers a kiss, a
sip of wine, a wafer pale as betrayal
　　　　　　　and many ways to turn away, and in his eyes hot rage
and terror of exile. I take him thoroughly in who stood and begged
before all doors – see what he makes of me –
　　　　　　　his gaze the veil which shimmering reveals the seen
to its own self, so that I tremble into life charged by asymmetry,
conceived in the Prophet's caress,
　　　　　　　　engendered mouth to mouth and born as difference
into this flesh. And given in a glance with wisdom of the wound comes
timid faith in frail undress
　　　　　　　with arms out-thrown to catch the nail or bless,
embrace with bloodied frown the one who searched:
　　　　　　　the perpetrator and the found.

VII
A Befalling

I creep into the stone circle and cast fresh offspring onto the moonlit plain.
I pitch it out at last to turn the tide that crawls and churning empties me
of all I am. Locked in the convulsion
        I hold fast to the sun and stars and they address me, saying:
You are ours. The earth rocks on her axis, splitting glacial height, sending
the sandstorm to raise dunes, conflating
        day and night. Take me, take me where small conceits,
the rosy remedies of cowardice and pride concocted to heal me of my need,
recede and are dispelled before immensities,
        asymmetries adorned with torque of twisted astral light
and fleeing spume of meteorite, dark floor weighed down in drowning,
crawled by worm lit from within
        that butts and shunts our past from cloudy reach to reach.
Take me to the breach whence creeps the tidal wave upon its course,
heaving upon its shoulder whale, off-cut
        of ice and never navigated flow. Brought to my knees
at last beneath the swell pressed hard upon the fontanelle, unguarded
diamond crown of liegeless king and clown –

        her feather fists in falling flay the air –

what very little grace we grant
        before she joins the fray, vernixed, still listening for
the higher heart, leaving in disarray this seat I thought a paltry place when
spewing gore in moonstruck heat
        it made of girlhood my disgrace.

VIII
Quasimodo

It's when he weeps the wildness wakes in me – the wailing that he makes,
it's not like mine. The beast
        in him coughs up gusts of grief – black corbie
cries that mount the magma red till far beneath us lies the rift, the bed,
the little death. I cower
        from his fractured face. I stare. What ravishment
is there? The towered keep is locked upon the hall, I watch the rocking
of the walls. Another mistress
        rides his chest, presses the anguish from his pores –

        where he breaks

        temperance beaks into being like a bird posing
as charnel child that wakes to night with fluttered lung and vellum
shuttered sight and uttering
        unearthly song. His bare nape awaits the breath
of blade, back bowed that bent to plough allows the flail, and in his side
the splinter rests
        like love, painlessly in the flesh. Such blundering
in extremis, sudden composure neither birth nor death – it robs the world
of doubleness, straight plot
        and scribe – leaves he replete with suffering and chary
of nomenclature, who shrinks from touch, afraid of tainting with reproach
sublime encounter
        clothed in awe.

IX

I ask him who he is, he says no
name embellishes his nakedness, not
now, not ever. Father, brother, he
whose hand homes uninvited to my
breast? He shakes his head. Earth lies
unpressed beneath his tread. Such
sorrow shrouds this place; the hour
devours its own shadow. He faints
upon his feet! How cravenly I waver,
how wantonly the rock hoards heat –
it sears low lesion scented yet
with myrrh and cauterises reason.

X
Strangers

Have, see and say is the gentile way, a pallor stalked by ambidextrous
sex. The going down
            of God has left us jousting with our genitals, no
call of honour bright abroad. Such blighted appetites, such maws! Where
is heart's seal,
            the guardian taboo that kept each faithful to
the tithe when she swooped with the sickle, he the scythe? What has
displaced the double thread
            and thrum and cast us loose like mumming fools,
feint wives riding our beauty like a mule? Some wayward following it was
begat pale Minotaur
            that fights and fucks and bares its bosom to the other
side roaring delinquent rights and due! More awful than the labyrinth
this harrowing, narrowing of the cell –
            the whiteness cannot find its face, but struts and gawps
at its own artifice –
            Look to your daughters, Magdalene, defiled,
midwifed by men, false messengers make eunuchs of us all, cavorting
the bought potter's field neutered amidst thistle and thorn.
            Listen, some humming winged things still crawl
a tumult filled with light in forlorn hunt for trill that leads back to the
hive or primeval decree, when tottering
            in latent lap, linked to the spark by milky way, with
limbs out-thrown and urgent plea newborn
            Astartes first yearned for her moon.

XI
Desiderata

Make me whole again. I am a milky pool held hard to winter forest's
heart. The birch dips her white toe in cloudy underskirts. How stiff
I grow. All the quiet
                    places locked in lull, aghast at their own dwindling,
ransack tomorrow for rare nurseries of wraiths, truant tumble and
wildwood wade, rough parting of the way where mooncalf gropes,
sleepwalking shade, for shrunken sun
                    clung round with hungry heliotrope. Little absences
crowd the glade – cowslip, mullein send sulphurous tirade from dimming
bank and soft as ever overstep the edge. Cradled in complicity, new loss
bereaves meadow and hedge,
                    and who will know bold Stramonium when night
terrors seize the bed, who bind physick and herb when destitution blinds
the world? Shake me sound again,
                    white child, you rush to meet me seeming to outrun
your age. Only orphan, your snowflake handprint brands the breast so
lately fled – you see,
                    no birthdays are remembered here (foundlings
swarm in your wake), no deaths, but every brow is smudged with sage.
Wake me, remake me, pity me…
                    the moon hangs captive in her monstrance as a lamb,
unleavened, lucid, lost for time,
                    awaiting alteration beyond blood and wine.

n'Bytsje

A seventh spring and still
I miss some arcane step
beside me through the wood,
while seedlings seek their secret
names you knew, and in the
quickening a tiny bride
trills her shy song in your
lost tongue – n'bytsje, n'bytsje –
how is she called who flitting
sweetens with her speech
the still that lies between
us now n'bytsje, how?

(Frisian: *n'bytsje [n-beet-tshi]:'a wee bit').*

Who by Water

I
relics

I left the forests for you, but you wanted more
from me. I did not know what, had never felt
that longing others have for nearness to the sea –

but now you throw trees in my path
and fight your way into my human
sloth, my human longing to be free,

you cast up debris at my feet like votive
offerings, rigor mortis of stem and ashy
sediment, land is your reliquary. So

sleek your curls wrung from the pool,
a girl puts up her hand to cold forehead
in feigned surprise, or vanity –

that being seen was what I did not know:
the vanquishing blank look that stares
beech back into her burnished

womb, that strips pine down to briny web
far-flung and hung with hostages. You
do not keep your promises, you keep

leaving. At first your hand lay light
on me, but soon I learnt the vigil
of the land, ebb tide, futility.

II
crossings

Sea-buried summer's cast-off trance
lies heaped like dreams of play where
footprints fill and day-danced turrets kneel –

you taught me this: to seasonally die
and take the salt for what it is, wisdom
even the wagtail learns, fraught acrobat

fording the creek, and that crossing may
be succinct in this starched levelling, stiff
reach for heaven and earth annulled

and doubly drowned, impartial laying
of the burden down on some far shore, so light, no
lighter cargo, from where the bar bites

at the tide with bare white teeth, hungering,
to dune-hid marsh that sighs, licks briny
lips scented with pine whose pulse runs

slow and dark as beat through peat-quenched
beast hard hunted down and steeped to stone
where Grass of Parnassus blows –

you keep the secrets that I seek, and are
always leaving. Do you remember me,
throwing yourself at my feet, weeping?

III
passage

I see what you mean, the burying,
the sucking clean of sand that leaves
a hand curled carefully to ear

listening (the way the child slept,
always with rapt attention for
the opening of a door) like all

the others abducted in the midst
of dream, conducted from the place
of suffering kaolin-lipped,

tongue-tied and haughty
as a blade-torqued queen –
there is no need to roar:

the day-shy fugist mounts her dais
again insisting on rehearsal, hauling
dirge after dirge towards the shore

recalling that which went before –
forgetting is all we ask,
but not so tethered a tide

that inadvertently the pulse
slides into that smooth quietus
too soon, too undiscerning.

IV
equus

You are not wary of the aftermath
but rush white-cheeked to fill
the river's narrow need, where

woman waters turn their backs on you,
dreaming of height, welter of white,
quartz crèche and in the spate

glancing caress of she who leaps
to lay and lay down her life. Yes,
some still know their way home

upstream, or flushed unshod from field
to shingle, kelpy noose sidled
loose till mane and tail

lie white along the wave again – they
were here long before us, small
when first they came ashore,

tip-toeing the tide, prancing, pawing
salt floor, leaving the ancestors to rear
and bow in perpetuity. It was inborn:

how to high-step the swell, breast
surpliced crest, turn shy cabochon gaze
guileless towards tomorrow.

V
white

Colder than hellebore
you chant the far hills
south from sleep

as though delay incensed you
and time lost waiting for the thaw
were mine, who doubts, builds

crumbling walls against spring
melt while marching cataracts
recall contract unbroken

since the fall – and curled like
ammonite in the curt clutch
of evermore I know

the small dry place we cling to
as summits crawl in self-ascent
for deposition by the stars

and fathoms far a madman
slips the lanyard on the mast,
missteps the deck

and in an ecstasy
of following and dread
sets foot beyond his terror.

VI
prophesy

And now you loop with lace
the red rock's riven face, ruffling
her cheek as since the dove

none has touched her,
and is it burn or is it blush
in headlong rush to bathe in blood

where evening's wine-glutted
priest throws back his head, sinks
to his knees at the straight meeting place –

smooth bed of star-limbed sleeper
lost from she who waited on the stair,
green sea-glass glance of he

who from the womb perceived
the nothingness of air and fled,
preferring anonymity – you keep

foretelling death of earth
unheard by master at the wheel
who shudders at the stifled stars

and savagery beneath the keel. Your law
is never mild where we are born,
your law is ravage.

VII
sophia

This was how you came before –
rough tongued tale-teller wild
as rain, shy prodigal of no

abode or name, vagrant voyager, woad
sailed son of she who brought
obedience to birth where day by day

we test oblivion, wandering barefoot
where the world ends, writing our name
in last light, gazing out to where

the shard-dashed alabaster heart husk
rides of every creature lost from flight,
caught in night net, downed by brine

clustered in the quill where only gimlet
sky should be – I have come to the very edge
where words are washed away

and am afraid for that sweet breath,
salt-milk suckled speak of death
by sea but not by drowning,

cold soliloquy of broken jade rinsed
of old servitudes and quietly dressed,
devoid of histories, unfinessed, proud.

Gull

Splay-winged, hang-limbed,
astounded as a hungry child
man-hoisted on the wind –

a scream of *take this cup*
from me sky-borne
above virtuous town

where fisherfolk bent the knee –
ravenous steeple-house lament
beside an emptied sea.

Waddenzee

1

Between glory and glory the
Meeting
Of untamed infinities
Bespeaking
In advancement and retreat
A land
Day dreamt, or dawn begotten
Bairn
Of sorrows spent in sleep,
Petulant
With waking pain,
Weeping
Unearthly lays wordless as
Spectra
Spread from dusk to shore
Recurring
In requiem until the solemn
Spoor
Of memory
Erase them

2

Recalling Time's full arabesque
As palls
Of light abate the breath,
Altering,
And rigid law foretells
A world
Stillborn in silvered caul
And day
And night dissemble
Retracing
Arctic step and all of life resembles
Loss,
But for the filigree flocked
Field
Blossoming like some enchanted
Sea
Where leaping siren danced and
Jade
Glass gives birth to sun-sung
Dynasty

3

Totems arise denoting
Solidarity
Withstanding turn of tide with
Tranquil
Tribe which searched the strand
Or fetched
A silver harvest home
Clasped
In the battened bosom
Between
White waters hungrier than they,
Older
And unperturbed by passage of slight
Prey
Spending its little life fallen
Between
Forever and today
Between
The heavens and
The clay

4

Builder of temples to
Maker
Without name who
Lays
To rest the molten sun and
Lifts
Life light from leaden deep and
Casts
Compassion on his world
In tones
No longer spoken. Gone the
Levy
Of salt and bread, the
Sultry
Offering, gone white and cold on
Lapsed
Bone broken altar – Behold!
His token
Of delight and parable of
Wonder

5

Come
Again, the word whispered from
Wave to
Wave or writ in wind upon the
Wing on
Every made and unmade
Thing
Dreaming its ageless
History
In moments of forgetting,
Lulled
By the poppy potion of the sun
Spilled
At the rim where tacit time
Works
All its transformations,
From fire
To flood and ushers in the quiet
Stone,
Mute, mesmerised by motion

6

Inchoate
The change inherent in each
State,
From shade to light a shifting tryst;
White
Blossom heads cast heaven high bow
Berried
Black to contemplate with bended neck
Anon
The modest place from whence they
Come
And all of loss makes way for
Gain
As wild with accession the seasons
Rush
To set their seal upon the day
Unmoved
By rival reason and every yearning void
Bears
Fruit as world-won wish is barren

7

And Man,
Beautiful in his bungling, moves
Through
His brief interval of much from
Want
To must, roaming the shore of
Infant
Lust unschooled even in his own
Might,
Strewing his petty detritus and waging war
Less great
Than cat on shrew or orchis flowering
Half-drowned
In inundated mead. Whilst where the
Banished
Silence waits his nets hang sweetly
Drying
And unvanquished the creed accrues,
Grave
Governance ever gathering

8

Always the swell of seed and
Shell,
The ravenous expanse stilled
In spiral
Catacomb, the husk refilled with earth
Forgot
Beside the riping furrow. How
Humbly rest
The remnants of our home
When
Life is fled and the ravaged spirit
Gone,
Recalled to elemental
Brine
Or to the complicated tomb.
Shall
We then grieve or dare to weep
Cast
Back upon the flowing shore
Once more?

9

Flooded with light the fertile
Plain,
Riven the waters in giving,
Untold
This legacy of golden day to each quiet
Remission
As ever and again the
Nascent
Dream slips into living –
First
Sleep falls in bewildered fold,
Erodes
Faltering sandy sprint, white
Burst
Of fire that lit the risen
Retina
At first-seen dawn, and taken
From us
Thus is bliss, forfeited in
Awakening

10

Maker and breaker of miracles,
Born
Fight-fisted lost and found
Labouring
Upon the ground, curled
In ear
Of corn, worn like
A frown
Upon the brow of beast
Blessed
In his own sightlessness:
None
Knew himself before thee –
See
The following, the fall, the unfurled
Rise
Of tides bearing abundantly
Bestow
Their untold bounty at
Your feet

11

Line
Traced pure from Pharaoh face, from
First
Contour to mark of kings,
Through
Ebb drawn trembling back from
Sibling dark
Edge carved in its own
Image
With neither start nor end in
Utmost
Secrecy, the evolution of the
Ledge,
Uncompassed path dissolved in
Loss,
So lost yet never straying,
Led
By some dictum of desire
Aloof
From promise and betraying

12

Turning
From salt to sweet the burden of
A sky
Tied to eternity by flickering
Fall
Of storm-fled bird, or swaying
Star
Scattering ecstasy like
Light
Upon the shattered wave and
Night
Drenching in dark his heaving
Nave,
Dragging his treasury of
Tears
Toward a shore sublime
As day
Divested of her pain to gaze
Unawed
As Aphrodite upon him

13

Hurling
Upon the infant head access
Bygone
Begotten, as if the sight of
Land
Aroused agony long forgotten
And rage
Engulfed the spark of grace
Swept
Into dim extinction in
Opalescent
Wept embrace bearing bearer and
Barren
In blind compulsion so to
Share
Before her hour grows older a
Legend
Rising in her womb too
Great,
Too hallowed for expulsion

14

And still
Untouched the lustrous world
As pearl
Unfolds in splendour and
None
Shall know the rendezvous of
Past,
Present and future, when
Warring
Wind shall cease and signal
Calm
Release the sign of
Peace
Above the meek inverted
Shell,
The gentle archipelago: swell-
Flown
Meeting-place where so
Supreme the
Dialogue of deference is spoken.

Tenebrae

Lapse

This is how it goes: the hare
prancing from long winter
into new green, the doe
through late bluebells
and early alkanet. We romp
through slipping seasons
like creatures
meant for mirth.

The man on the train with doctor's
hands reads biography
as though his life
depends on it. We are
creatures of death
and birth but each
prefers another's.

The silversmith who at her father's
knee learnt malleability,
abandons her moon metal
priced beyond her reach
and carves instead
in wood or stone
egret, a woman
and a man.

We are all older. The potter's kiln
is crammed with cul-de-sacs
and paths that all lead
back. The only way we know
is clay. She too has lost
her faith. Decades pass

through our simple
solitudes like beads,

in the silversmith's face
pale stabat mater.

Child martyrs

Solstice – gulls scull
pools of stagnant sleep,
fill northern night's
short parenthesis
with prayer, parade
on bare pink scalloped
feet, yelp at the door
for pity, go
tippety-toe like
child martyrs –

we never learn, but wake
to dread, turn, stumble
from the room. They are
watching from behind the moon
till chance admit them

raggedy hemmed, cuffs
bitten, gauffered grey, cloud
gownies trailed through
corridors of sky, wide
sleeves sucked clean
of salt and tide…

they lift their chins and scream.
These complaints are untrue. We
did not do these things.

Reciting our misdeeds like mischief
saved for private play, half-night
brings them scolding
and deriding down

upon us wielding
knives and swearing
God is great.

We should be lost without
them. War is nothing
to us: a little wait
where the air seethes,
where the dust breathes
and death is made easy.

Vigil

The hour of occlusion
discovers us rehearsing
utmost loss, full
of presentiment
and pride we find
the ward from which
he just now took
his leave, the empty
bed, a common stair,

bare atrium of welcome
and farewell, thin
hour of passing
through

high-stepped by blue-
eyed murdering man-
cat who like a wave
capsized his plumy
prey, left her
moon-eyed
marooned
by the door,
clay-oared
and songless

dawn does not mourn
but idles innumerate among
the come and gone
light bringers
while

the cribbed sea weeps
itself from sleep to sleep

Milk Bay

'Mamma is nie meer 'n mens nie'
Ingrid Jonker (1933-1965)

Watch, my daughter, how the tide
   hides its mutability, glides
      hushed in lovers' arms from ebb to flow…

the night I felt you breast womb water, tip slow
   somersault, anemone brush
      my floating rib, I knew to call you sea-moan,

sea-sure, something not like me – take care
   my sweetling, my heart, and don't go
      in too far, never above your middle, Mamma

used to say, before her words turned whiter
   than wing lightening, *ma cheri,*
      bright flickering above Milk Bay. I was a starfish

cast from salmon-bellied cloud-clasp down
   between dune grass and wrack
      and in the shark-fin shadow of the rocks

made a sand hole for my precious things, quartz
   and conch and green sea
      glass, but my friend would not come and see,

'Later,' he said, 'later,' and over and again
   the tumbled tide dismissed us
      with its promises, threw us its 'perhaps'

and 'when' until the river mouthed him free,
   wrapping his tulip hips
      with weed, his face a sip of sea-mare milk

and saltspeak on his lips. Listen, my crimson-hearted
one, my lamb, take care, the men
are monsters here, beware cheap secrets

breathed into your hair, kisses that dumbfound
your mouth, as silver-clappered
as a bell – fetch your bucket and spade – look,

a yellow moon lies on its back between
a shell-strewn heaven
and the galaxy-skimmed wave! All day we've played,

but mummy madness is a game I cannot win…
wanting too rife, too near
a daughter and too far a wife… see how

the shore wears water's frown? It's not the dark man,
darling, you must fear, but he
whose pallor weighs upon him like a crown.

I lay between black promises
and the whiteness of their lies,
it was baptism by desire, I would not learn,

they could not love my wildness or my rhymes. Stay
safe, daughter, above the brim…
frilled pennants lift, silk streamers fill Milk Bay,

I dream salt-sequinned Spartacus unbound
and gentle as the dawn and yes
and yes he says and draws me roaring down.

Winter's Child

I

      Who craves comfort? I, who dreams
day drench to dismay night's chapelled lay,
amaze chill east with newness, who once knew
the way back through absence of the word, slow
fledgling fall of late-laid bird and evening's
shy icon face lit with departing kiss of light,
honey-suckled moon rising
              to dawn's rainbow breath of herb
come to bathe unready day, calm nurse without
commotion, emotionless as some chaste child's
request for gravitas that unmasks the god-lost past
heart hurtle in retreat from sudden unasked
glory, as though some fey presentiment foretold
enchantment's story ending in sleep lulled far too deep,
steep down from orchard slope to trout-brown
stream thrush-touched and feathered
ferny green as summer's bracken hide or lost
in wave-wept wood strummed by May rain.

II

       Who still plays two-ball against the wall
of that cold crèche where time lies catacombed,
cradled white as stalagmite, where blood blended
in brotherhood we scrawled our truth, called names
along the labyrinth, listened in dread for
the footfall that meant discovery?
       Who did not count the pulse amiss in pale
parental temple, a beat long lost from angel
fall, not tremble; who not mouth a savage waif
sentence of sin upon the dolls'-house world
of men that broke our pact with mystery,
the seal that made us more than mortal?

III

Be still girl-soul within your carapace
of stone! Night's shy anchoress has wed you
to herself and soon your small unhungry womb
will feel its famish for vermillion, filigree
fingers reach for vagrant moons. Who heard
tomorrow come?
Bees hung beneath clustered lime-tree
suns stunning with honeys a dolorous
and deedless sky. After rain the thirst-quenched
heath loosed hosts of Tutankhamen butterfly, kholed
aureoled in gold, and aphis born to sip and die –
swift and forlorn this mantling
of the meadow, gashed grass, spilled eye,
scythed stem, cloud shadowed requiem.

IV

   Who knows the old day-darkened
way? Though lustrous light lay in her face
and her bird breath stilled flute-trilled stars.
We may not follow yet. Clasping our ragged
souvenirs, the careless gift, the crude uneven
epithet, we bear the fading note that pierced
the pleasure of our days, the shared awakenings
of midnight feasting far too soon and tolled in
playmateless the hours from dusk till noon,
when carved in beech we find the long-loved
name, twin truant sweetheart loved again.

V

   Who knows whom to turn away? Too late
to unlock the cottage gate, rue angelus thrice rung,
chance thrice missed for sacrifice –
   master alone and shivering beneath night's
silvered olive bough, bruise-heeled among dream-
waltzers at the dance, listening for the split hiss, soft
glistening moon-begotten kiss upon the brow –

VI

how have I come again to this? dull orphan
of forgetting, son of same sundered tribe
eager as ever for the trance, keen for the cup
as for the bribe to bless the cull of cousin

(remember and remember he
who fights with reason, who
gentles war with a blunt sword
and gives pity her season)

VII

Who fled the field? I, ebb-eyed worrier
flood-limbed and friendless, who seeks another
wounded self at the torn edge of asylum, where
I stare aghast at my own past, wry warrior faint
with fear, knee-deep in sea-grass asking where
walks the cogent healer.

Where hero heart reverts to green
beneath dawn's wrung ungoverned sky, where
learning is undone and larch bends low to brush
our faces as we run wanting and not wanting
to know, afraid and unafraid to go through
annulment and snow towards the ceaseless
chapterhouse, spectra-drowned habitat of stone
engraved with rapturous parable in nave and
architrave and throne and barefoot child arrival.

Yellow Sampan

It is a long time since I have seen you, Li Po.
A pity that you have feigned madness –
The whole world would have you die,
But my heart dotes on your gifted soul...
                                    Tu Fu (A.D. 713-770)

Tall and strong as young bamboo, my son
Stands in the stern of the yellow sampan.
As it leaves the jetty he waves to me,
Out on the balcony among butterflies.
Tiny birds flutter in late summer's trees.

Dai Lin

Dai Lin, named for New Year,
Rests her chin on my knee, claims
This long day in company. One paw
On my arm detains me while she dreams.
A cat turns an hour into eternity.

Forest

In the forest the wild boar sleeps
Suckling her young in shade.
Perfumed, the path gives birth
To red flowers, trefoils, ferns,
Rests in afternoon's warm lap.

Fisherwoman

Early the fisherwoman rows out
Into the bay, flings her net into jade.
Her shirt like pink peach blossom
Follows the moving water. Her boat
A turquoise dragonfly poised on its bows.

White Crane

Blue waters lap the old pontoon
Moored on morning motionless.
When the white crane alights
He catches only his own shadow,
Flashing like a paper fish.

Women of Canton

The women of Canton are strong.
All day she works, rows, hauls nets,
Weighs anchor, roars across the bay,
Recalls the matriarchs who captained
Pirate ships, watches and has her say.

Yellow Dog

Today I am well enough to explore
The forest path. I set out alone, afraid,
Alert for snakes. The warm damp air
Is scented with trees. A yellow dog
Has followed me from the village.
Yesterday I feared him. Now
He keeps me safe, nose down
Shows the way, turns, pauses, waits.

Temple of the Sea Goddess

In the village temple, old boat shed,
Paper lanterns float above the altar,
Golden flowers and bells adorn her,
Red tassels garland the shrine, gifts,
Incense and lights for safe harbour.

Port Shelter

As if painted on a jade silk fan
The mountains flatten their peaks
Against the sky, their flanks
Thickly forested and green.

At their feet small rocky coves
Enclose this hidden bay
Which for a thousand years
Fishermen have called home.

Over the path hang red flowers,
Beneath the pier fishes thread
Silver silk through water weft,
Anemones cling to stone.

My son is a man now and knows
His place on sea and land, seeks
His own course by the stars, sails
Out far from our old home.

Banyan Tree

In Sai Kung's park an ancient banyan drops
Its thousand rusty arms to embrace the dusty earth,
Raises its sacred crown to root itself in grace,
Holds to its old heart our few green years.

Little Pier

The old planks of the little pier
Are rotten and awry. Venture out
Over turquoise water. At the end
Sit and dip your toes into warm sea.

Kite

Above the far mountain a kite
Soars, hangs on wings wider
Than the sky. From his heaven
He can see the huntress leave,
Her whelp stumble from the lair.

Seasons

This morning mist hides the mountains,
The butterflies that clattered like jewels
In the trees are gone, green leaves grow dull.
Soon the rains come and summer dies.

Bougainvillea

On my first day in Ma Nam Wat we walk
The paved path up from the jetty between
High white walls. Suddenly a pack of pale
Dogs swarms down the hillside to meet us.

Bright pink bougainvillea subdues my terror.
My son greets the barking dogs, 'Hello boys!'
Beside the path a tiny shrine, trefoil, three
Terracotta bowls, stone Buddha, seated, calm.

Lady Butterfly

Round the headland sails Lady Butterfly,
Proudly her small prow skims the sea.
A warm breeze in her white silk wings
Brings her into the bay to salute me.

Behind her on the hills a new campus
For learning, the towering island city.
In wind and water is written the way
Of all things, past, present and to come.

To the Poet

I have journeyed to your land at last, Li Po,
Come ashore on the far southern seaboard.
As a young girl I flew on your winged words,
Now I am old, but my heart is free as a bird.
I will sing your songs along the paved path
Through the ancient village, past tile-roofed
Cottages of fishermen, along the forest trail.

The green mountains are as you left them
And the wine tastes the same. Each morning
I meet you, tall as a tree, refilling your cup,
Maned jet black, phoenix poet, fiery, fearless
As the sun. For sixty-six years I have sought
The chaste soul's radiance, come home to your
Truth: 'The world hates a thing too pure'.